Gramma: Kyroeeee
Kyroe: Yes, Gramma
Gramma: are you ready for your big day?
 Kyroe: Yes, Gramma, my 1st day at school. It's going to be so exciting and I'm going to get to meet new friends.

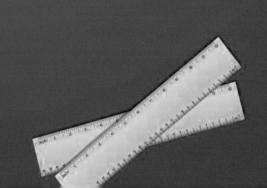

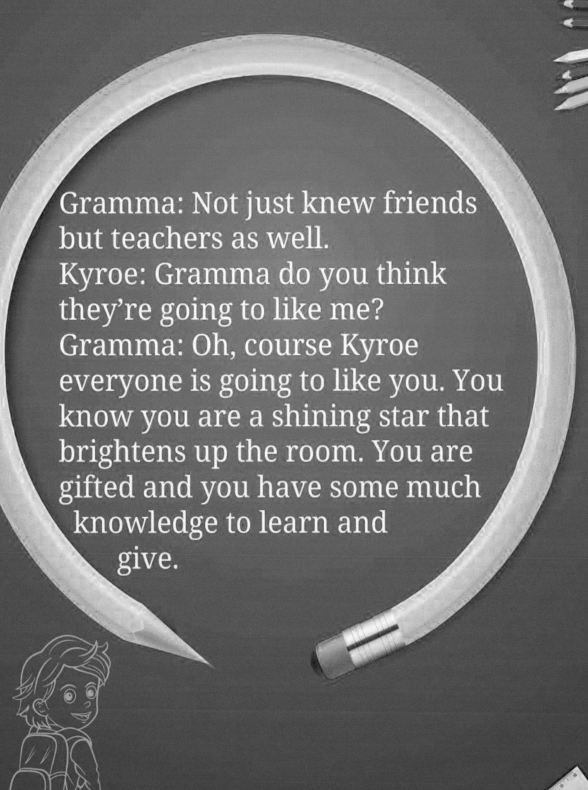

Gramma: Not just knew friends but teachers as well.

Kyroe: Gramma do you think they're going to like me?

Gramma: Oh, course Kyroe everyone is going to like you. You know you are a shining star that brightens up the room. You are gifted and you have some much knowledge to learn and give.

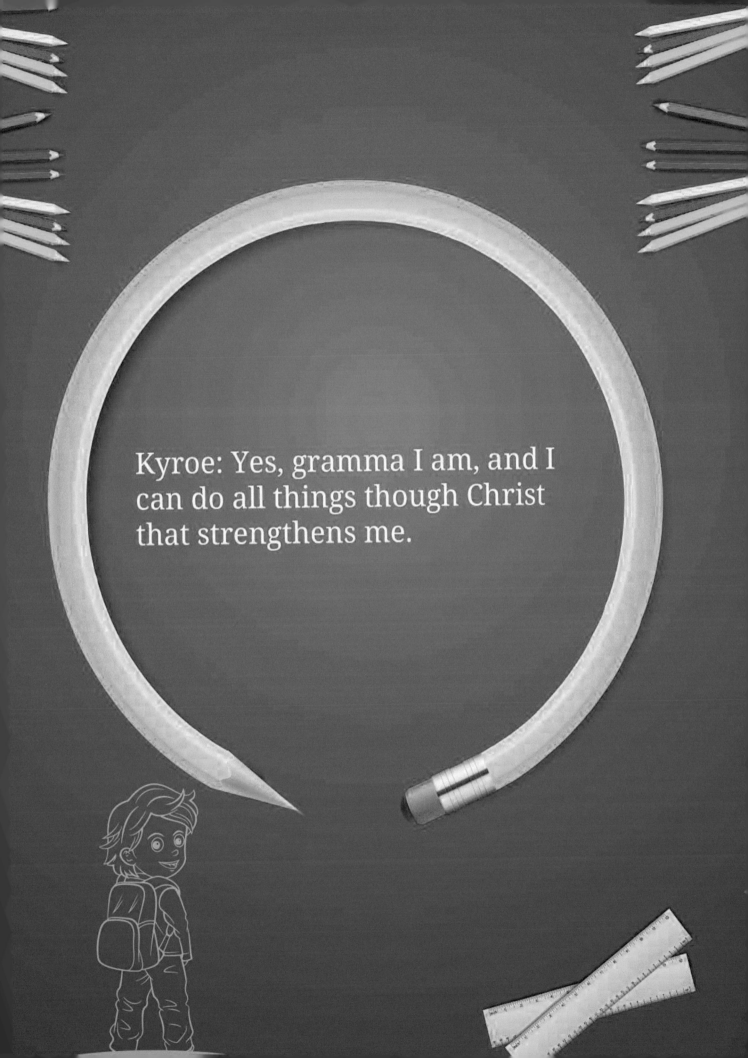

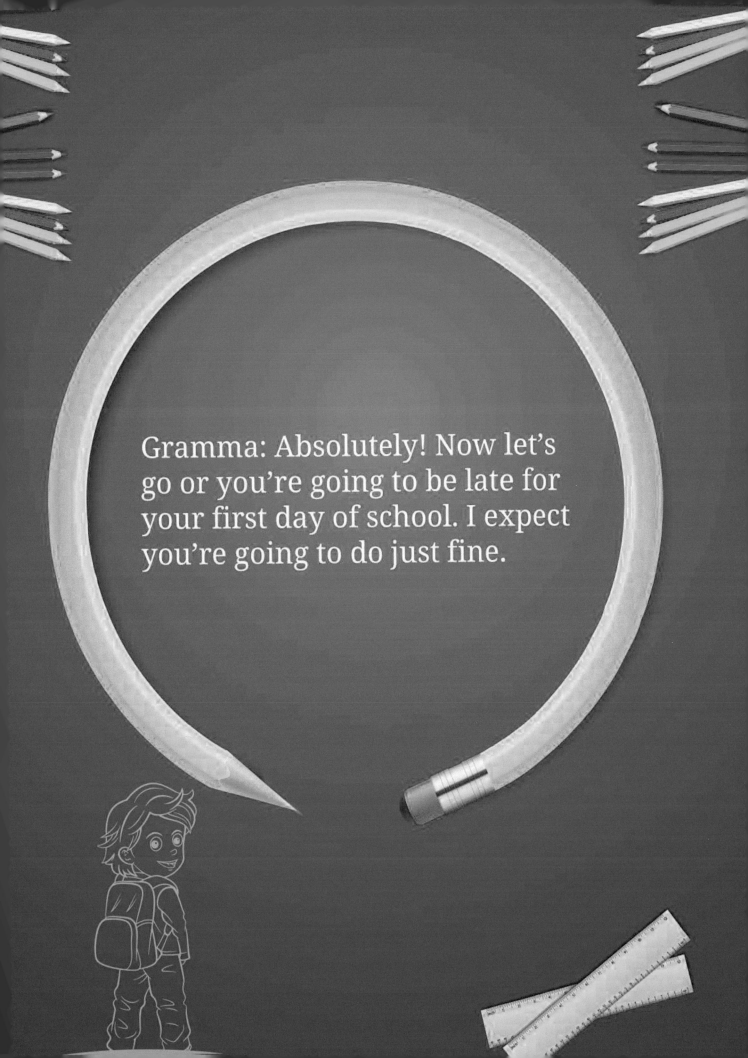

Gramma: Absolutely! Now let's go or you're going to be late for your first day of school. I expect you're going to do just fine.

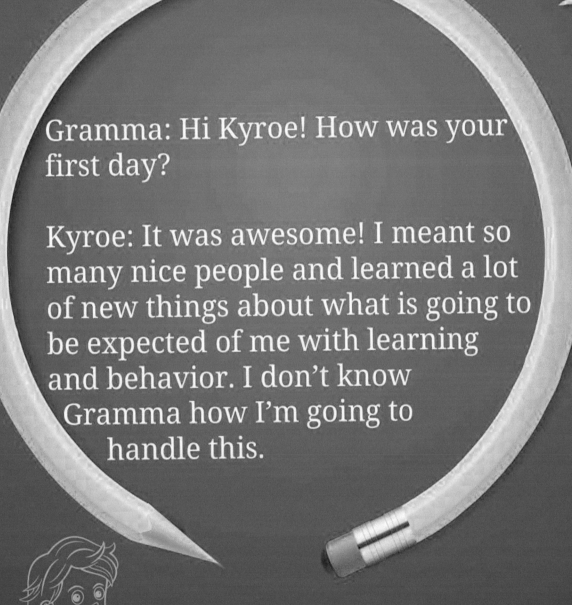

Gramma: Hi Kyroe! How was your first day?

Kyroe: It was awesome! I meant so many nice people and learned a lot of new things about what is going to be expected of me with learning and behavior. I don't know Gramma how I'm going to handle this.

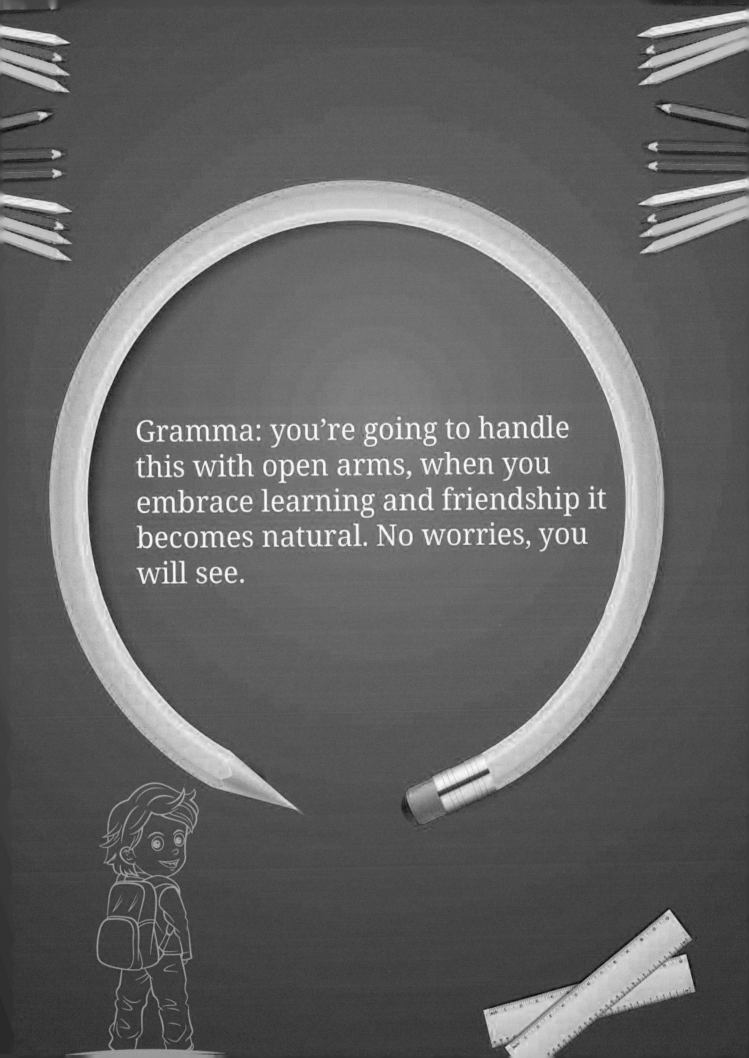

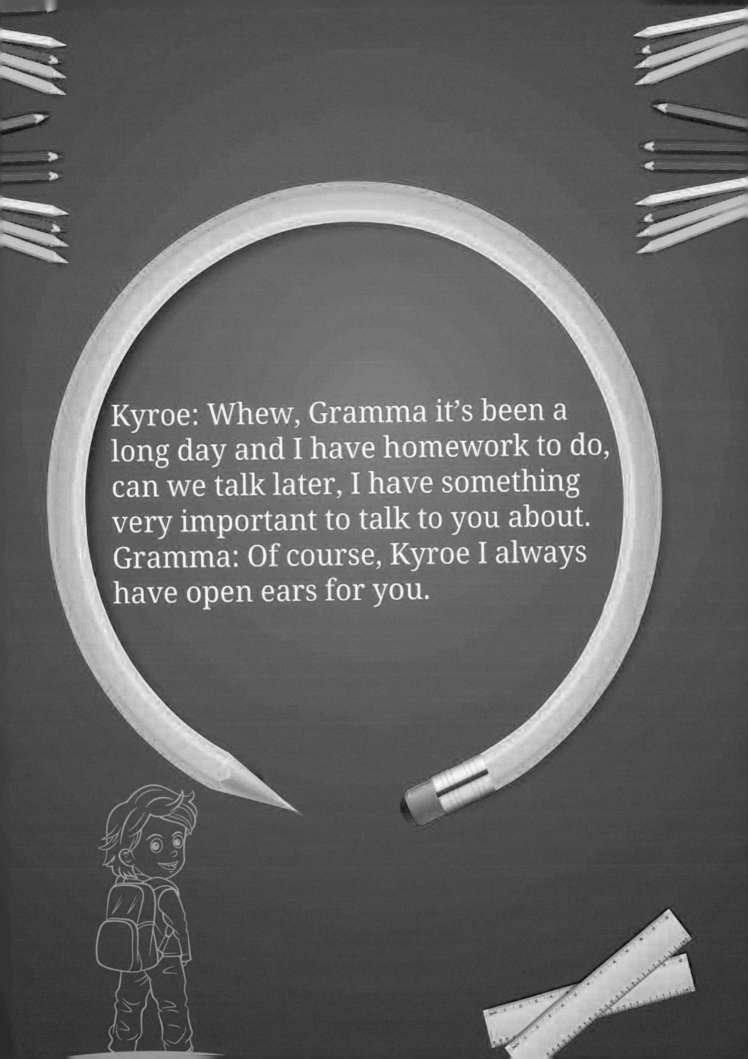

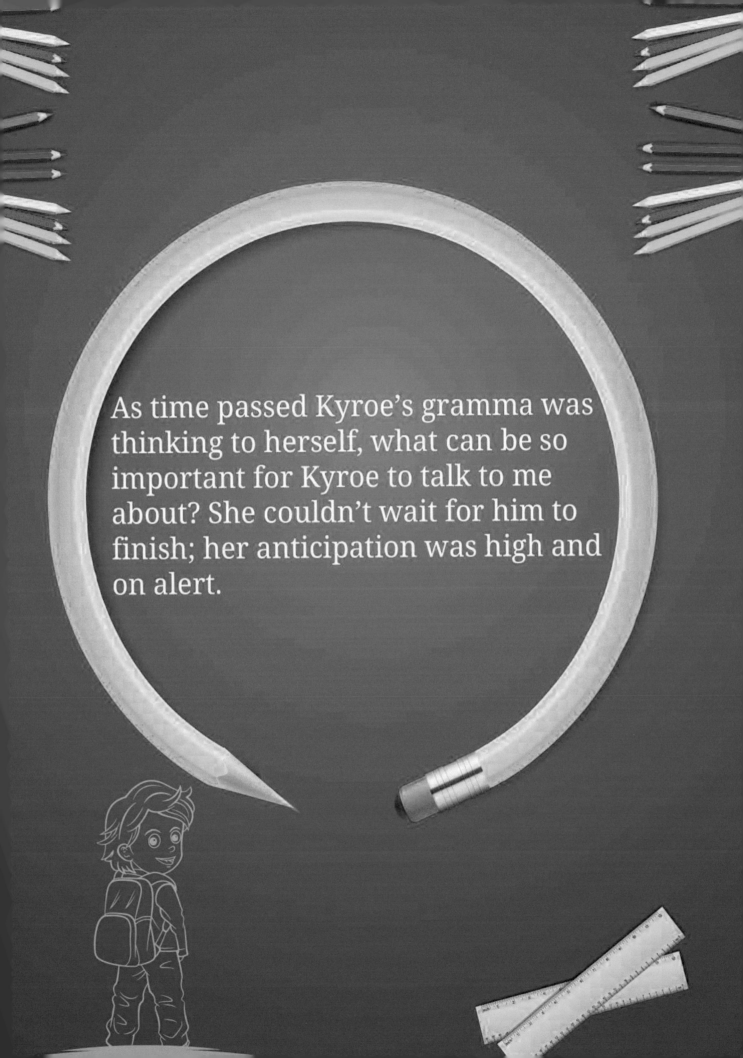

As time passed Kyroe's gramma was thinking to herself, what can be so important for Kyroe to talk to me about? She couldn't wait for him to finish; her anticipation was high and on alert.

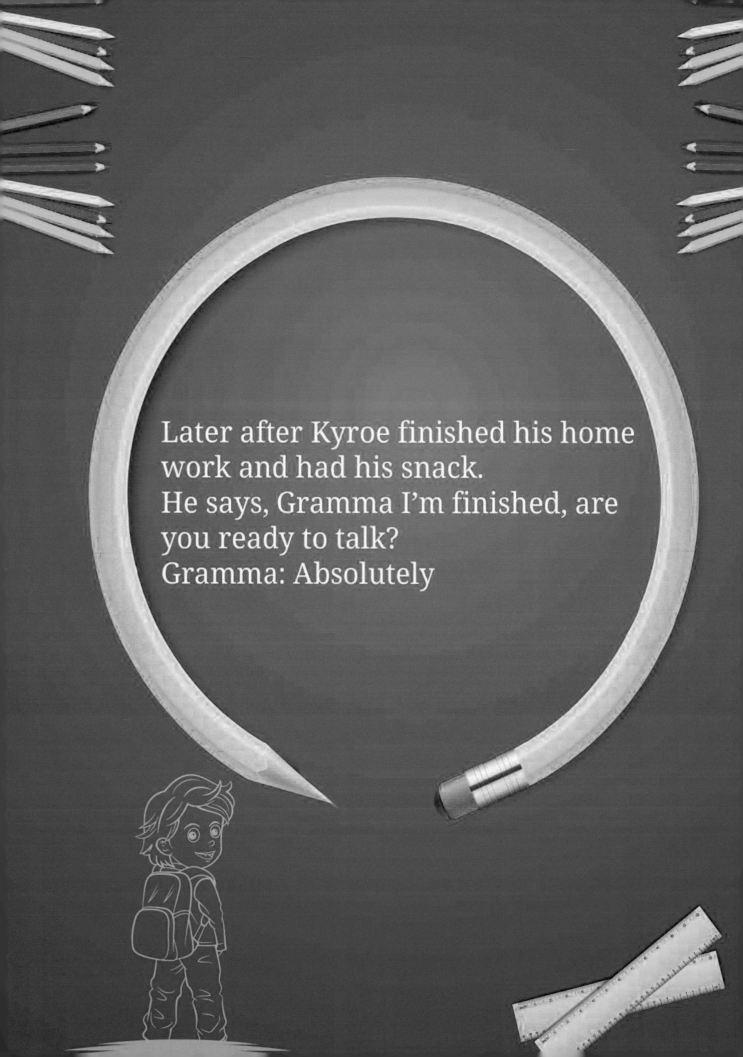

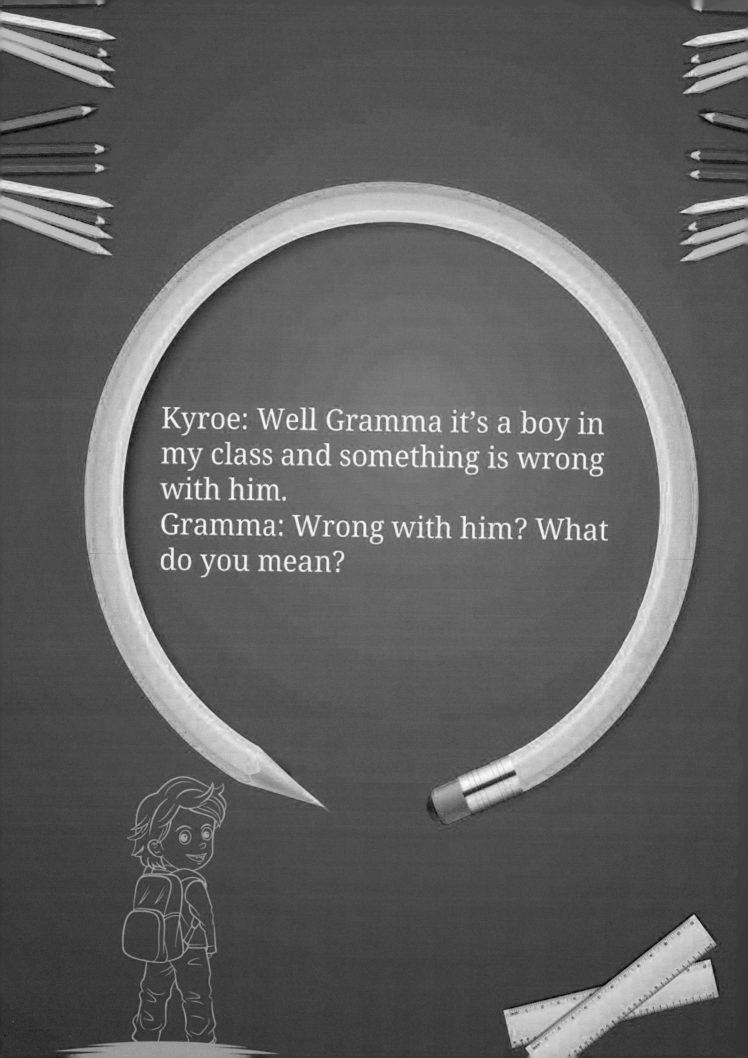

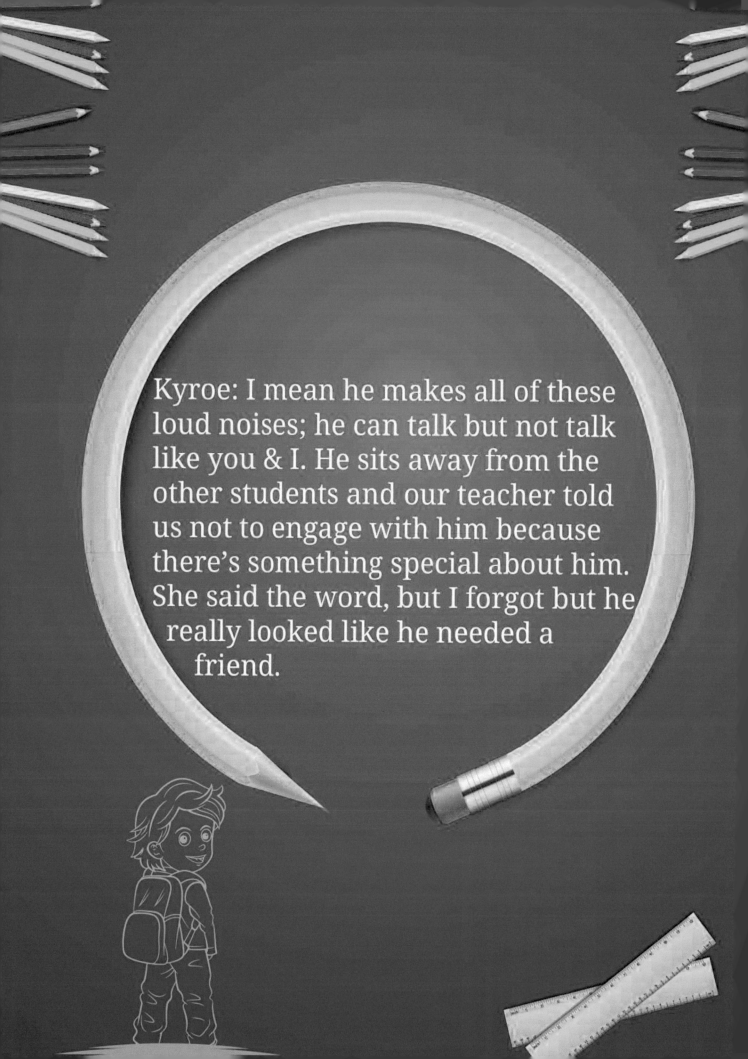

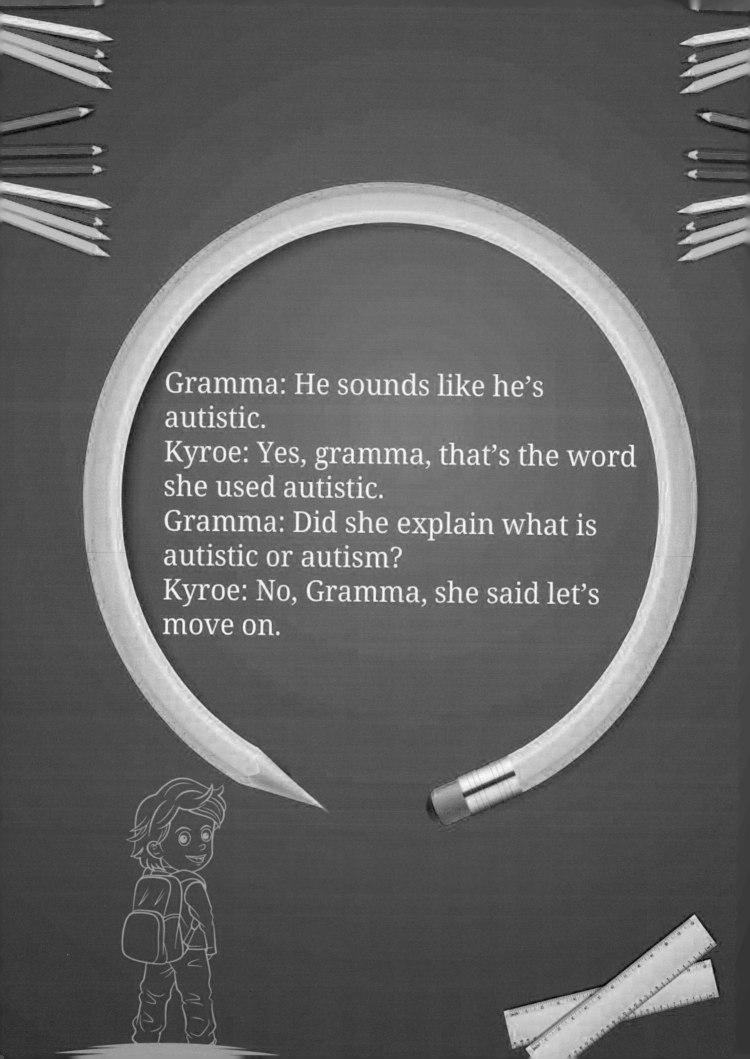

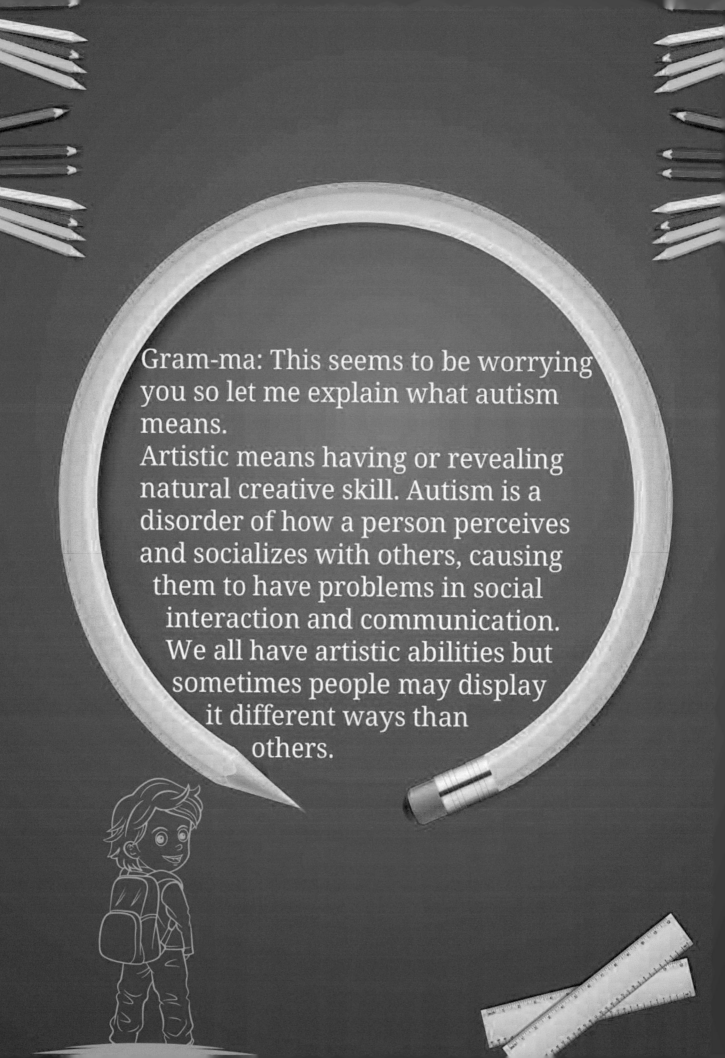

Gram-ma: This seems to be worrying you so let me explain what autism means.
Artistic means having or revealing natural creative skill. Autism is a disorder of how a person perceives and socializes with others, causing them to have problems in social interaction and communication. We all have artistic abilities but sometimes people may display it different ways than others.

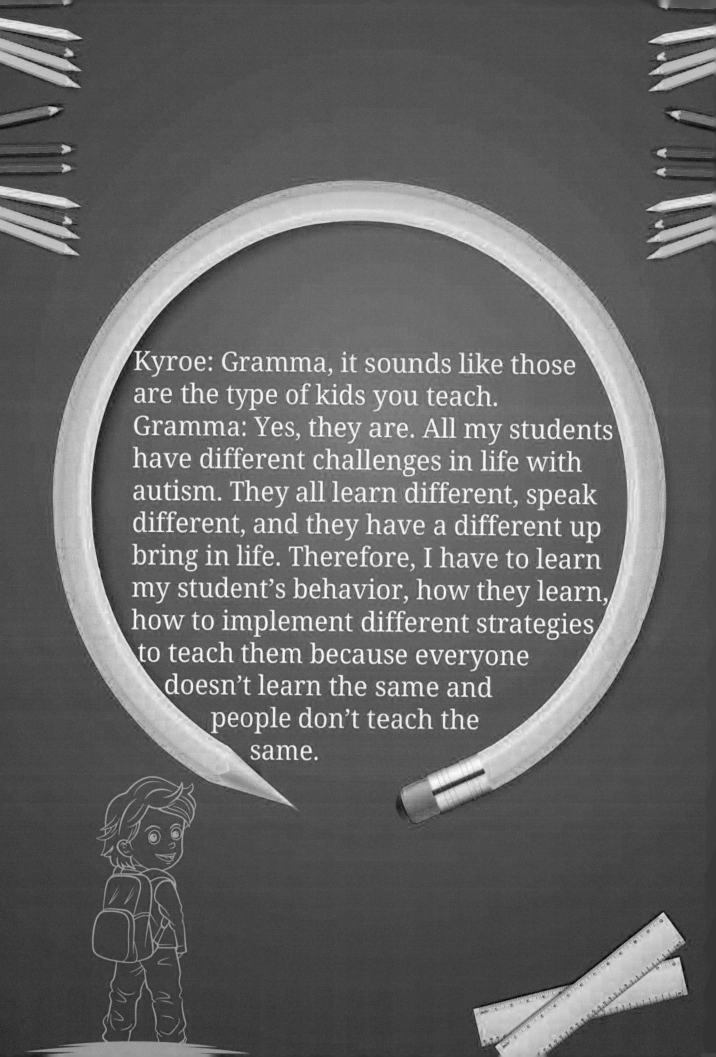

Kyroe: Gramma, it sounds like those are the type of kids you teach.

Gramma: Yes, they are. All my students have different challenges in life with autism. They all learn different, speak different, and they have a different up bring in life. Therefore, I have to learn my student's behavior, how they learn, how to implement different strategies to teach them because everyone doesn't learn the same and people don't teach the same.

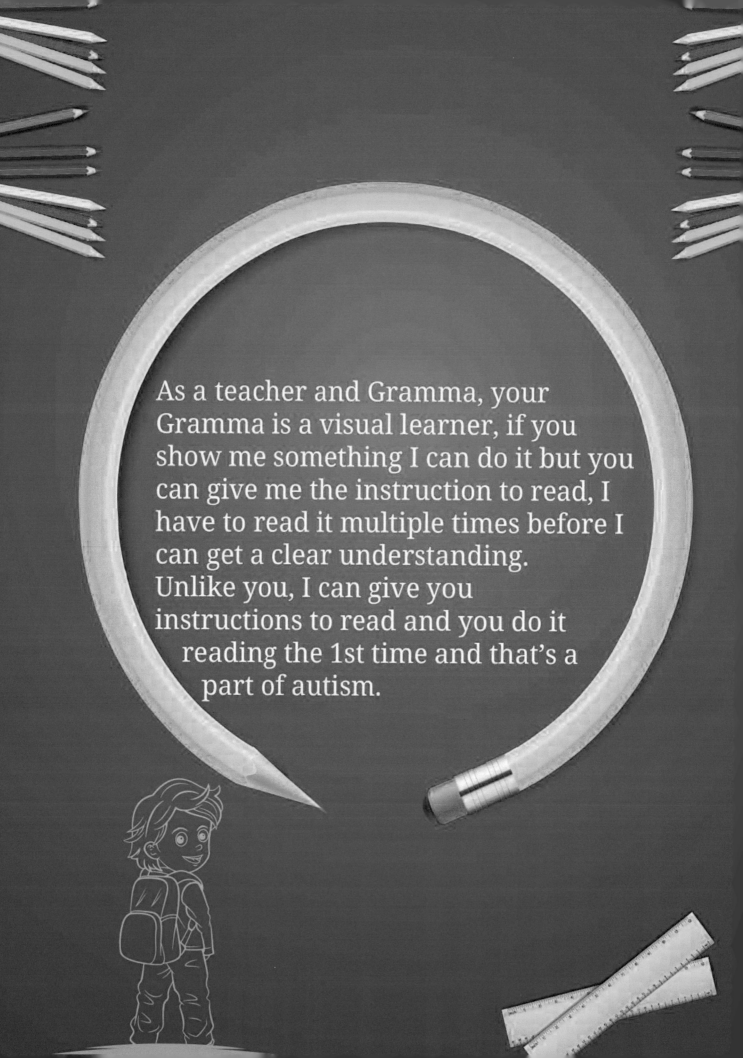

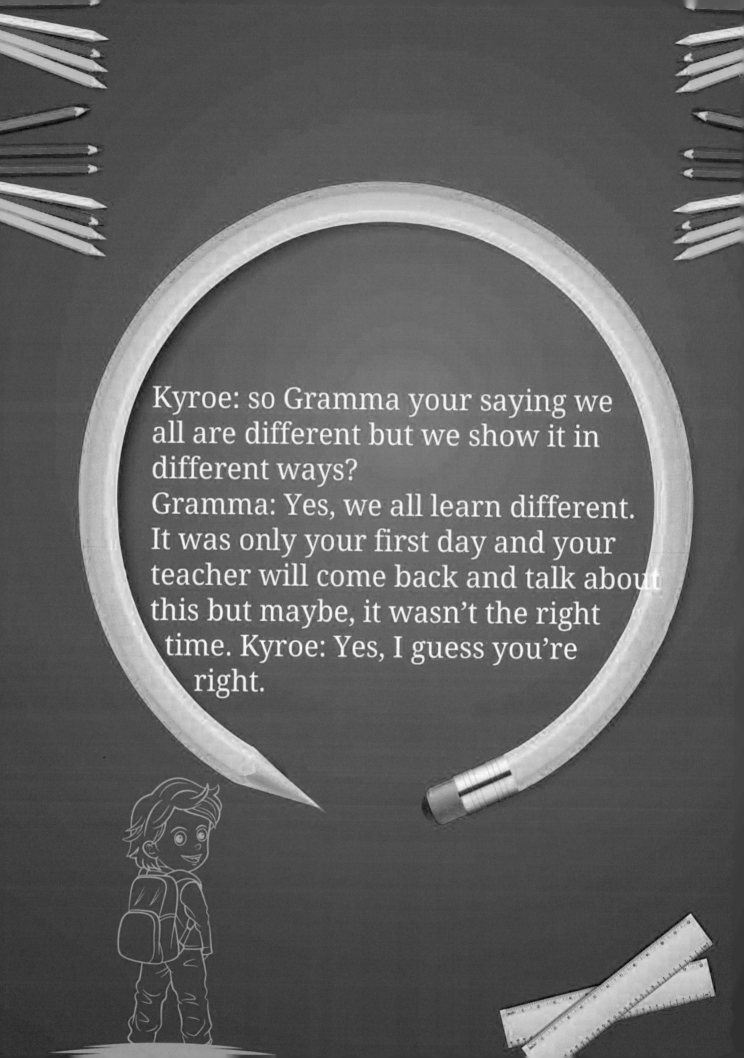

Kyroe: so Gramma your saying we all are different but we show it in different ways?

Gramma: Yes, we all learn different. It was only your first day and your teacher will come back and talk about this but maybe, it wasn't the right time. Kyroe: Yes, I guess you're right.

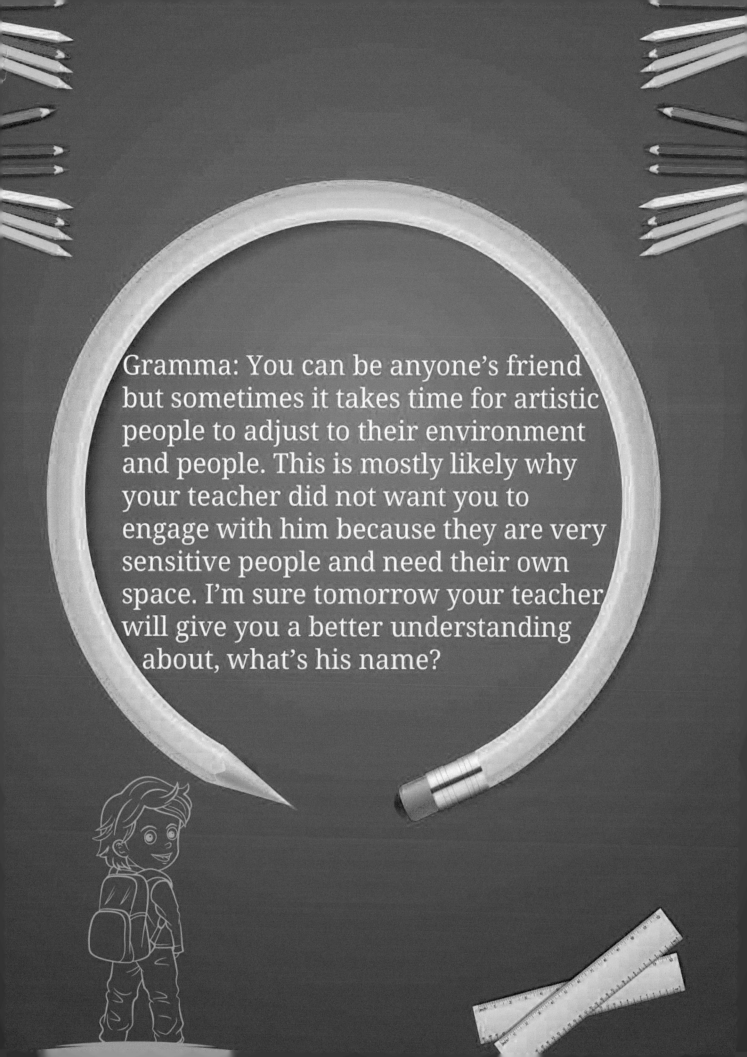

Gramma: You can be anyone's friend but sometimes it takes time for artistic people to adjust to their environment and people. This is mostly likely why your teacher did not want you to engage with him because they are very sensitive people and need their own space. I'm sure tomorrow your teacher will give you a better understanding about, what's his name?

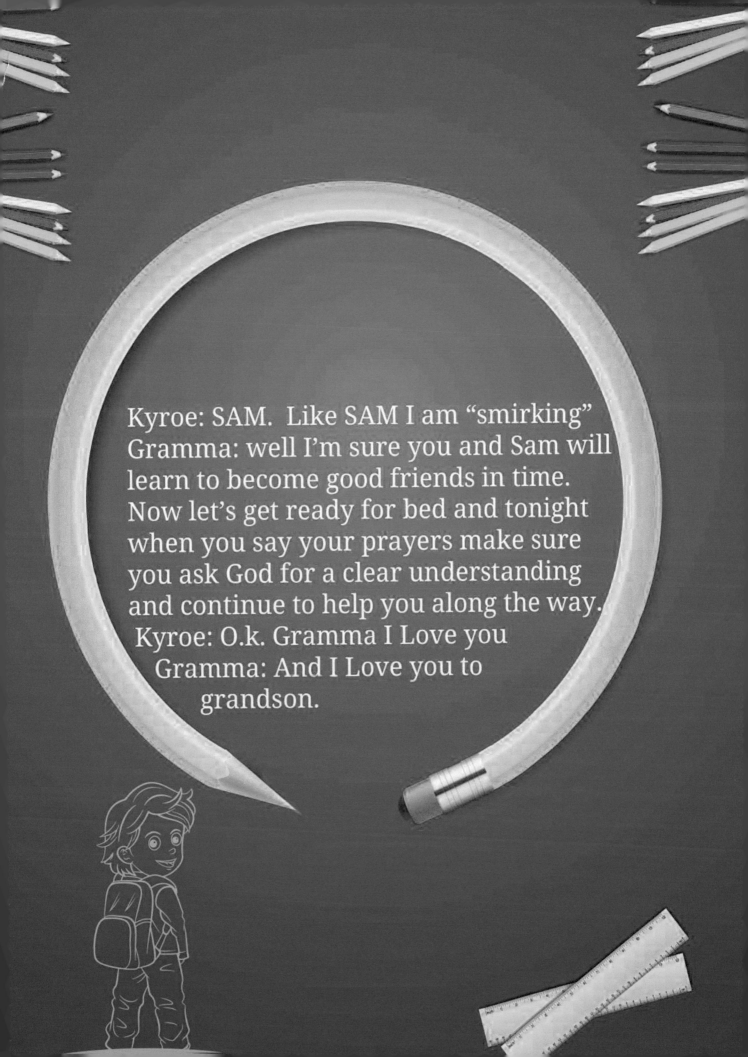

Kyroe: SAM. Like SAM I am "smirking" Gramma: well I'm sure you and Sam will learn to become good friends in time. Now let's get ready for bed and tonight when you say your prayers make sure you ask God for a clear understanding and continue to help you along the way. Kyroe: O.k. Gramma I Love you Gramma: And I Love you to grandson.